BELGR

TRAVEL GUIDE

2024

Discovering Belgrade: Navigate the City Like a Local with Our Expert Recommendations.

BY

ALFRED CHAPMAN

All rights reserved. No part of this publication may be reproduced, distributed, or transmitted in any form or by any means, including photocopying, recording, or other electronic or mechanical methods, without the prior written permission of the publisher, except in the case of brief quotations embodied in critical reviews and certain other noncommercial uses permitted by copyright law.

This book is a work of nonfiction, and while every precaution has been taken in the preparation of this work, the author and publisher assume no responsibility for errors or omissions, or for damages resulting from the use of the information contained herein. The views and opinions expressed in this book are those of the author and do not necessarily reflect the official policy or position of any other entity.

This book is intended to provide general information and is not a substitute for professional advice. The author and publisher disclaim any liability for any loss or risk incurred as a consequence of the use and application, directly or indirectly, of any content in this book.

Copyright © 2024 by Alfred Chapman

Table of Contents

Table of Contents 2

Introduction 5

    Overview of Belgrade 7

    History of Belgrade 9

    Geography and Climate 11

CHAPTER 1: Getting to Belgrade 13

    Transportation Options 13

    Arriving by Air 15

    Arriving by Train 17

    Arriving by Bus 19

    Getting Around the City 22

CHAPTER 2: Accommodation 25

    Types of Accommodation 25

    Hotels 27

    Hostels 30

    Apartments 32

CHAPTER 3: Exploring Belgrade 37

    Belgrade's Neighborhoods 37

Top Attractions 39

    Kalemegdan Fortress...41

    Skadarlija 43

    St. Sava Temple 45

    Ada Ciganlija 48

Museums and Galleries 50

Parks and Gardens...52

CHAPTER 4: Eating and Drinking in Belgrade 55

Traditional Serbian Cuisine 55

Popular Restaurants and Cafes..57

Street Food 61

Nightlife 63

CHAPTER 5: Shopping in Belgrade 67

Markets and Bazaars..67

Shopping Districts 69

Souvenirs and Gifts..72

CHAPTER 6: Day Trips from Belgrade 75

Novi Sad 75

Sremski Karlovci 77

Vojvodina..80

    Šumadija Region...82

CHAPTER 7: Practical Information......................................87

    Language and Communication 87

    Currency and Money Matters...89

    Safety Tips..92

    Etiquette and Customs 95

CHAPTER 8: Events and Festivals 99

    Belgrade Beer Fest..99

    Belgrade Music Festival (BEMUS)....................................101

    EXIT Festival 103

CHAPTER 9: Further Resources 107

    Useful Websites...107

    Useful Apps..113

Conclusion 117

Introduction

Welcome to the Belgrade Travel Guide! Whether you're a first-time visitor or a seasoned traveler to the Serbian capital, this comprehensive guide is your go-to resource for experiencing all that Belgrade has to offer.

Situated at the confluence of the Sava and Danube rivers, Belgrade is a city with a rich history, vibrant culture, and an undeniable charm. From its ancient fortress to its bustling city streets, Belgrade encapsulates a unique blend of tradition and modernity, making it a captivating destination for travelers from around the globe.

In this guide, we'll take you on a journey through the winding streets of Belgrade, uncovering its hidden gems, iconic landmarks, and local secrets. You'll discover the city's diverse neighborhoods, each with its own distinct character and allure. Whether you're exploring the historic streets of Stari Grad or soaking up the bohemian atmosphere of Skadarlija, Belgrade promises an unforgettable experience at every turn.

We'll delve into Belgrade's rich cultural tapestry, from its fascinating museums and galleries to its vibrant culinary scene. Get ready to tantalize your taste buds with mouthwatering Serbian cuisine, sample the finest rakija in town, and dance the night away in Belgrade's legendary nightlife hotspots.

But Belgrade isn't just about what lies within its city limits. We'll also guide you on exciting day trips to nearby destinations, where you can explore medieval monasteries, tranquil countryside, and charming towns steeped in history.

Whether you're planning a short city break or an extended stay, this guide is your passport to unlocking the heart and soul of Belgrade. So pack your bags, grab your camera, and get ready to embark on an adventure of a lifetime in one of Europe's most dynamic and captivating cities. Welcome to Belgrade – we're thrilled to have you here!

Overview of Belgrade

Historical Significance:

Belgrade's history is marked by a series of conquests, wars, and transformations, leaving behind a tapestry of architectural styles and cultural influences. From its origins as a Celtic settlement to its time under Roman, Byzantine, Ottoman, and Austro-Hungarian rule, Belgrade has witnessed the rise and fall of empires, shaping its identity as a resilient and dynamic city.

Modern Capital:

Today, Belgrade is a vibrant metropolis that reflects both its storied past and its aspirations for the future. The cityscape is a blend of ancient fortresses, neoclassical buildings, socialist-era blocks, and modern skyscrapers, showcasing its diverse architectural heritage.

Cultural Melting Pot:

Belgrade is known for its thriving arts and cultural scene, with numerous museums, galleries, theaters, and music venues scattered throughout the city. From classical performances at the National Theatre to avant-garde exhibitions at the Museum of Contemporary Art, there's no shortage of cultural experiences to explore.

Cosmopolitan Flair:

As the largest city in Serbia, Belgrade is a melting pot of cultures, languages, and traditions. Its diverse population reflects the city's openness and cosmopolitan spirit, creating a dynamic and welcoming atmosphere for visitors from all walks of life.

Dynamic Nightlife:

Belgrade is famous for its vibrant nightlife, with a plethora of bars, clubs, and cafes that cater to every taste and preference. Whether you're sipping cocktails on a floating river club, dancing until dawn in a converted warehouse, or enjoying live music in a cozy jazz bar, Belgrade offers endless opportunities for evening entertainment.

Natural Beauty:

Despite its urban hustle and bustle, Belgrade is blessed with abundant green spaces and natural beauty. From the sprawling Kalemegdan Park to the picturesque Ada Ciganlija island, there are plenty of opportunities to escape the city and reconnect with nature.

History of Belgrade

Ancient Origins:

Belgrade's history dates back to ancient times, with evidence of settlements dating as far back as the Neolithic period. The area was inhabited by various tribes and civilizations, including the Celts and the Romans, who established the fortress of Singidunum in the 1st century AD.

Medieval Period:

In the Middle Ages, Belgrade became a significant fortress town in the Byzantine Empire and later the Kingdom of Hungary. It was conquered and reconquered numerous times by various powers, including the Bulgarians, Byzantines, and Serbs. The Serbian Despotate established its capital in Belgrade in the 15th century, marking the beginning of the city's prominence in the region.

Ottoman Rule:

In 1521, Belgrade fell to the Ottoman Empire after a prolonged siege, marking the start of over three centuries of Ottoman rule. During this time, Belgrade flourished as an important Ottoman provincial center, with the city's population growing significantly and its culture and architecture influenced by Islamic and Ottoman traditions.

Habsburg and Austrian Rule:

Belgrade was briefly liberated from Ottoman rule in the late 17th century by the Habsburg Monarchy but was returned to Ottoman control in 1739. However, in the early 19th century, Belgrade once again came under Habsburg rule as part of the Serbian Revolution against Ottoman rule. It was later incorporated into the newly formed Principality of Serbia.

Modern Era:

The 20th century brought significant changes to Belgrade, including two World Wars and the breakup of Yugoslavia. During World War I, Belgrade was occupied by Austrian and German forces and suffered extensive damage. In World War II, the city was bombed heavily by the Axis powers.

Capital of Yugoslavia:

After World War II, Belgrade became the capital of the Socialist Federal Republic of Yugoslavia. Under the leadership of Josip Broz Tito, Yugoslavia pursued a policy of non-alignment and became a prominent player on the world stage.

Contemporary Belgrade:

Following the breakup of Yugoslavia in the 1990s, Belgrade became the capital of the newly formed Federal Republic of

Yugoslavia and later the Republic of Serbia. Today, Belgrade is a dynamic and cosmopolitan city, with a thriving cultural scene, vibrant nightlife, and a growing economy.

Despite its turbulent history, Belgrade has emerged as a resilient and vibrant metropolis, where traces of its past can be found at every corner, from its ancient fortress to its elegant boulevards and historic neighborhoods.

Geography and Climate
Geography:

Belgrade is located in the north-central part of Serbia, occupying a prominent position on the Balkan Peninsula. The city is characterized by its varied topography, with the flatlands of the Pannonian Plain to the north and the hilly terrain of the Balkan Peninsula to the south.

The cityscape is dominated by the confluence of the Sava and Danube rivers, which form a natural boundary between the Old Town (Stari Grad) and the New Belgrade (Novi Beograd) districts. The iconic Kalemegdan Fortress sits proudly atop a cliff overlooking the confluence, offering panoramic views of the city and its surroundings.

Climate:

Belgrade experiences a continental climate with distinct seasons, influenced by its inland location and proximity to the rivers. The summers are typically hot and humid, with average temperatures ranging from 20°C to 30°C (68°F to 86°F). July is the warmest month, often seeing temperatures exceeding 30°C (86°F).

Winters in Belgrade are cold and snowy, with average temperatures ranging from -3°C to 5°C (27°F to 41°F). January is the coldest month, with temperatures occasionally dropping below freezing. Snowfall is common during the winter months, creating picturesque scenes across the city.

Spring and autumn are characterized by mild temperatures and transitional weather conditions. These seasons are ideal for outdoor activities and exploring the city's parks, gardens, and outdoor attractions.

Belgrade receives moderate precipitation throughout the year, with slightly higher rainfall in the spring and autumn months. Thunderstorms are common during the summer, providing relief from the heat and humidity.

CHAPTER 1: Getting to Belgrade

Transportation Options
Public Transport:

Bus: Belgrade has an extensive bus network operated by GSP Beograd, covering most parts of the city and its outskirts. Tickets can be purchased onboard or at kiosks, and routes are well-marked.

Tram: Trams provide another convenient mode of public transportation in Belgrade, running along major thoroughfares and connecting various neighborhoods.

Trolleybus: Trolleybuses are electric buses powered by overhead wires. They operate on specific routes, offering a clean and efficient way to travel around the city.

Belgrade Metro:

As of the writing of this guide, Belgrade is in the process of constructing its metro system, which will provide a rapid transit option for commuters and travelers. While the metro is not yet fully operational, it is an exciting development for the city's transportation infrastructure.

Taxi Services:

Taxis are readily available throughout Belgrade, offering a convenient way to travel door-to-door. It's advisable to use licensed taxi companies or reputable ride-hailing apps to ensure fair pricing and reliable service.

Bicycles and Scooters:

With the introduction of bike-sharing schemes and electric scooter rentals, cycling and scooting have become popular options for short trips around the city. Many dedicated bike lanes and paths make cycling a safe and enjoyable way to explore Belgrade.

Walking:

Belgrade's compact city center makes it highly walkable, allowing visitors to easily explore its streets, parks, and landmarks on foot. Walking is often the best way to soak in the city's atmosphere and discover hidden gems off the beaten path.

Car Rental:

For those who prefer the freedom of having their own vehicle, car rental services are available in Belgrade. However, it's important to note that traffic congestion and limited parking in the city center can make driving challenging, especially for first-time visitors.

Water Transport:

Belgrade's location at the confluence of two major rivers, the Sava and the Danube, offers opportunities for water transport. While not as commonly used for daily commuting, boat tours and river cruises provide a unique perspective of the city and its waterfront.

Arriving by Air
International Flights:

Belgrade Nikola Tesla Airport is well-connected to major cities across Europe, Asia, and beyond, with numerous airlines operating regular flights to and from the airport. Major carriers such as Air Serbia, Lufthansa, Turkish Airlines, and Aeroflot serve the airport, providing travelers with a wide range of options for international travel.

Terminal Facilities:

The airport has two terminals – Terminal 1 and Terminal 2. Terminal 1 primarily handles domestic flights and low-cost carriers, while Terminal 2 is used for international flights. Both terminals offer a range of facilities and services, including shops, restaurants, currency exchange offices, car rental agencies, and VIP lounges.

Transportation from the Airport:

Upon arrival at Belgrade Nikola Tesla Airport, travelers have several transportation options to reach the city center and other destinations:

Taxi:

Taxis are readily available outside the terminals, and they provide a convenient way to reach your destination in Belgrade. Make sure to use authorized taxi services and agree on the fare with the driver before starting your journey.

Airport Bus:

The A1 minibus service operates between the airport and the city center, with stops at key locations such as Slavija Square and the main bus and train stations. The journey takes approximately 30-40 minutes, depending on traffic conditions.

Car Rental:

Rental car services are available at the airport for travelers who prefer to explore Belgrade and its surroundings at their own pace. Several international and local car rental companies have desks located in the arrivals area of the terminals.

Private Transfers:

For a hassle-free arrival, you can arrange a private transfer in advance to take you from the airport to your accommodation in Belgrade. Many hotels and travel agencies offer this service, allowing you to travel in comfort and style.

COVID-19 Measures:

In light of the ongoing COVID-19 pandemic, Belgrade Nikola Tesla Airport has implemented various health and safety measures to ensure the well-being of passengers and staff. These measures may include temperature checks, mandatory mask-wearing, increased cleaning and disinfection protocols, and social distancing guidelines. Travelers are advised to check the latest travel advisories and entry requirements before planning their trip to Belgrade.

Arriving by Train

International Train Services:

Several international train routes connect Belgrade to neighboring countries and major European cities. These routes include trains from Budapest, Vienna, Sofia, Thessaloniki, Zagreb, and Bucharest, among others.

International trains typically arrive at Belgrade Main Railway Station, providing passengers with a convenient gateway to the city.

Domestic Train Services:

Belgrade serves as a hub for domestic train travel within Serbia. The city is connected to various destinations across the country, including Novi Sad, Niš, Subotica, and other major cities and towns. Domestic train services offer travelers an affordable and efficient way to explore different regions of Serbia.

Facilities at Belgrade Main Railway Station:

Belgrade Main Railway Station is equipped with facilities and amenities to enhance the travel experience for passengers. These include ticket offices, waiting areas, luggage storage facilities, restrooms, and cafes or snack bars. Information desks are also available to assist travelers with inquiries regarding train schedules, ticket prices, and other travel-related information.

Transportation from the Railway Station:

Upon arriving at Belgrade Main Railway Station, travelers have several transportation options for reaching their accommodations or exploring the city further. Taxis, buses, and tram services are readily available outside the station, providing convenient connections to various parts of Belgrade. Additionally, many hotels are located within walking distance or a short ride from the railway station, offering easy access for arriving passengers.

Travel Tips:

It's advisable to purchase train tickets in advance, especially for international journeys or during peak travel seasons, to ensure availability and secure preferred seating.

Check train schedules and departure times in advance, as they may vary depending on the day of the week and the specific route.

Keep valuables secure and be vigilant of your belongings while traveling on trains and at railway stations, particularly in crowded areas.

Arriving by Bus
Belgrade Bus Station:

The Belgrade Bus Station is the primary hub for intercity and international bus services. Situated on the outskirts of the city center, the station is easily accessible by public transportation, taxi, or on foot from certain parts of the city.

Domestic and International Routes:

The Belgrade Bus Station serves both domestic and international routes, making it a convenient gateway for travelers arriving from neighboring countries such as Croatia, Bosnia and Herzegovina, Montenegro, Hungary, and Bulgaria, among others.

Facilities and Services:

The bus station offers a range of facilities and services to accommodate travelers, including ticket offices, waiting areas, restrooms, luggage storage, cafes, and shops. Information desks are also available to assist passengers with inquiries and travel arrangements.

Timetables and Tickets:

Timetables for bus departures and arrivals can be found online, at the station, or through various travel agencies. It's advisable to book your tickets in advance, especially during peak travel seasons, to secure your seat on preferred routes.

Transportation Options:

Upon arrival at the bus station, travelers have several transportation options to reach their accommodations or desired destinations within the city. Taxis, public buses, and ride-sharing services are readily available outside the station, providing convenient access to different parts of Belgrade.

Navigating the Station:

The Belgrade Bus Station can be bustling, particularly during peak hours. It's recommended to arrive early for departures and allow extra time to navigate the station, purchase tickets, and locate your platform or bus bay.

Accessibility:

The bus station is equipped with facilities to accommodate passengers with disabilities or special needs. Ramps, elevators, and accessible restrooms are available to ensure a comfortable experience for all travelers.

Safety and Security:

Like any transportation hub, it's essential to remain vigilant of your belongings and surroundings while at the bus station. Keep valuables secure, be cautious of potential scams or pickpocketing, and follow any posted safety guidelines.

Getting Around the City
Public Transportation:

Bus: Belgrade has an extensive network of bus routes that cover the entire city and its outskirts. Tickets can be purchased directly from the driver or at kiosks.

Tram: Trams are another popular mode of transportation in Belgrade, especially for traveling within the city center. They offer a convenient and affordable way to reach various attractions and neighborhoods.

Trolleybus: Trolleybuses are electric buses that run on overhead wires. They operate on specific routes and are a reliable means of getting around Belgrade.

Metro: While Belgrade does not have a metro system yet, plans for its development are underway. Currently, there are proposals for the construction of several metro lines to improve public transportation in the city.

Taxi Services:

Taxis are readily available throughout Belgrade and can be hailed on the street or booked through various taxi companies. Make sure to use licensed taxis with clearly displayed rates to avoid overcharging.

Ride-hailing apps like Uber and Bolt are also operational in Belgrade, providing additional convenience and transparency in pricing.

Bicycles:

Belgrade is increasingly becoming more bike-friendly, with dedicated bike lanes and rental services available throughout the city. Cycling is a great way to explore Belgrade's streets while enjoying the sights and sounds at your own pace.

Walking:

Many of Belgrade's attractions are within walking distance of each other, especially in the city center. Walking allows you to immerse yourself in the city's vibrant atmosphere and discover hidden gems along the way.

Renting a Car:

If you prefer the flexibility of having your own vehicle, car rental services are available in Belgrade. Keep in mind that traffic in the city can be congested, especially during peak hours, so plan your routes accordingly.

River Transportation:

With the Danube and Sava rivers flowing through Belgrade, river transportation offers a unique way to see the city from a different perspective. River cruises and boat tours provide a relaxing way to explore Belgrade's waterfront and iconic landmarks.

CHAPTER 2:
Accommodation

Types of Accommodation

Hotels:

Belgrade boasts a wide selection of hotels ranging from budget-friendly options to luxurious five-star establishments. Whether you're looking for modern amenities, spa facilities, or panoramic views of the city, you'll find a hotel to meet your needs. Many hotels are centrally located, making it convenient to explore Belgrade's top attractions.

Hostels:

Ideal for budget-conscious travelers and backpackers, hostels in Belgrade offer affordable accommodation in shared dormitories or private rooms. Hostels often provide communal spaces, such as lounges or kitchens, where guests can socialize and connect with fellow travelers. Some hostels also organize activities and tours to help you make the most of your stay in Belgrade.

Guesthouses and Bed & Breakfasts:

For a more intimate and personalized experience, consider staying at a guesthouse or bed & breakfast in Belgrade. These establishments typically offer cozy accommodations in a homelike setting, with friendly hosts who can provide insider tips on exploring the city. Guesthouses and bed & breakfasts are often located in residential neighborhoods, offering a glimpse into local life.

Serviced Apartments:

Perfect for travelers seeking a home away from home, serviced apartments in Belgrade provide the convenience of self-catering accommodation with the amenities of a hotel. These fully furnished apartments come equipped with kitchens, living areas, and often include services such as housekeeping and concierge assistance. Serviced apartments are an excellent option for families, groups, or long-term stays.

Airbnb and Vacation Rentals:

With the rise of platforms like Airbnb, travelers have access to a wide range of vacation rentals in Belgrade, including apartments, houses, and even unique accommodations like houseboats or lofts. Renting a private home or apartment allows you to experience Belgrade like a local, with the flexibility to cook your meals and live at your own pace.

Boutique and Design Hotels: For those seeking a unique and stylish accommodation experience, boutique and design hotels in Belgrade offer curated spaces with distinctive decor, personalized service, and attention to detail. These smaller, independently-owned hotels often showcase local art, design, and craftsmanship, providing a memorable stay that reflects the city's creative spirit.

Hotels
Luxury Hotels

Metropol Palace, A Luxury Collection Hotel: Situated in the heart of Belgrade, this iconic hotel combines timeless elegance with modern luxury. With its opulent rooms, gourmet dining options, and world-class amenities, Metropol Palace promises an unforgettable stay for discerning travelers.

Square Nine Hotel Belgrade: Boasting sleek design and impeccable service, Square Nine Hotel offers a sophisticated retreat in the heart of the city. Guests can indulge in Michelin-starred dining, relax in the spa, and enjoy panoramic views of Belgrade from the rooftop terrace.

Hyatt Regency Belgrade: Located overlooking the scenic Sava River, Hyatt Regency Belgrade offers contemporary comfort and unparalleled hospitality. With its spacious rooms, extensive wellness facilities, and convenient location, it's the perfect choice for both business and leisure travelers.

Boutique Hotels

Hotel Moskva: A beloved landmark in Belgrade, Hotel Moskva exudes old-world charm and elegance. Dating back to 1908, this iconic hotel offers luxurious accommodations, exquisite dining options, and a prime location near some of the city's top attractions.

Envoy Hotel Belgrade: Nestled in the trendy Dorćol neighborhood, Envoy Hotel is a stylish boutique hotel that combines modern design with personalized service. With its cozy rooms, vibrant atmosphere, and rooftop terrace offering panoramic views of the city, it's a favorite among savvy travelers.

Jump INN Hotel Belgrade: With its hip design, vibrant colors, and quirky decor, Jump INN Hotel offers a unique boutique experience in the heart of Belgrade. Guests can enjoy comfortable rooms, a lively bar, and a warm, welcoming atmosphere that captures the spirit of the city.

Budget-Friendly Accommodations

Hostelche Hostel: Located in the bohemian Skadarlija district, Hostelche Hostel offers budget-friendly accommodations in a lively and social atmosphere. With its colorful dorms, friendly staff, and central location, it's the perfect choice for backpackers and budget travelers.

Hostel Bongo: Situated near the bustling Republic Square, Hostel Bongo provides affordable accommodations with a cozy and welcoming atmosphere. Guests can enjoy comfortable dorms, a communal kitchen, and helpful staff who can provide insider tips on exploring the city on a budget.

Sun Hostel: Conveniently located near the train and bus stations, Sun Hostel offers clean and comfortable accommodations at budget-friendly prices. With its laid-back vibe, helpful staff, and convenient amenities, it's a popular choice for travelers looking to save money without sacrificing comfort.

Hostels

Hostel 1

Location: Centrally located near Republic Square

Facilities: Dormitory-style rooms, private rooms, communal kitchen, common area with TV, free Wi-Fi, 24-hour reception

Atmosphere: Lively and social, great for meeting fellow travelers

Additional Services: Organized city tours, bike rental, airport shuttle

Hedonist Hostel

Location: Nestled in the bohemian Skadarlija district

Facilities: Stylish and modern décor, mixed and female-only dorms, private rooms, rooftop terrace, bar, free breakfast, free Wi-Fi

Atmosphere: Relaxed and cozy, perfect for solo travelers and couples

Additional Services: Pub crawls, walking tours, laundry facilities

Downtown Belgrade Hostel

Location: Situated in the heart of Belgrade's downtown area

Facilities: Clean and spacious dorms, private rooms, fully equipped kitchen, common lounge area, free tea and coffee, free Wi-Fi

Atmosphere: Friendly and welcoming, ideal for travelers seeking a central location

Additional Services: Bike rental, luggage storage, airport transfers

Sun Hostel

Location: Located in the lively Dorćol district, close to Kalemegdan Fortress

Facilities: Colorful and vibrant décor, mixed and female-only dorms, private rooms, terrace with city views, bar, free breakfast, free Wi-Fi

Atmosphere: Energetic and sociable, with nightly events and activities

Additional Services: City tours, pub crawls, 24-hour reception

El Diablo Hostel

Location: Set in the hip and artistic Savamala neighborhood

Facilities: Funky and eclectic design, mixed and female-only dorms, private rooms, communal kitchen, garden terrace, bar, free Wi-Fi

Atmosphere: Bohemian and laid-back, with live music and cultural events

Additional Services: Bicycle rental, BBQ nights, airport transfers

Apartments
Types of Apartments:

Studios: Ideal for solo travelers or couples, studios typically offer a compact living space with basic amenities.

One-Bedroom Apartments: Perfect for small families or groups of friends, one-bedroom apartments provide a separate sleeping area along with a living room and kitchen.

Two or Three-Bedroom Apartments: For larger groups or families, these apartments offer multiple bedrooms, bathrooms, and ample living space.

Penthouse Apartments: Luxury seekers will find penthouse apartments with stunning views, high-end furnishings, and exclusive amenities.

Locations:

City Center: Apartments in the heart of Belgrade offer easy access to top attractions, restaurants, and nightlife hotspots.

Vračar: This residential neighborhood boasts tree-lined streets, cozy cafes, and proximity to attractions like the St. Sava Temple.

Dorćol: Known for its historic charm and bohemian vibe, Dorćol is a popular choice for those seeking a vibrant atmosphere.

New Belgrade: With its modern high-rises and waterfront promenades, New Belgrade appeals to travelers looking for a contemporary setting.

Amenities:

Fully Equipped Kitchens: Many apartments come with kitchens equipped with essential appliances and cookware, allowing guests to prepare their meals.

Wi-Fi and Entertainment: Most apartments offer free Wi-Fi access, along with amenities like flat-screen TVs, DVD players, and stereo systems.

Air Conditioning and Heating: To ensure a comfortable stay year-round, apartments in Belgrade are equipped with air conditioning for the summer months and heating for the winter.

Booking Options:

Short-Term Rentals: Many apartment owners offer short-term rentals, making them ideal for travelers planning a weekend getaway or a week-long stay.

Long-Term Rentals: For those looking to immerse themselves in Belgrade's culture and lifestyle, long-term rental options are also available.

Booking Platforms:

Airbnb: Airbnb offers a wide range of apartments in Belgrade, from budget-friendly options to luxurious accommodations.

Booking.com: Booking.com features a variety of apartments in Belgrade, along with guest reviews and convenient booking options.

Local Agencies: Some travelers prefer to book directly through local agencies or property managers, offering personalized service and assistance.

CHAPTER 3: Exploring Belgrade

Belgrade's Neighborhoods

Stari Grad (Old Town):

Stari Grad is the heart of Belgrade, where the city's rich history comes to life. Here, you'll find iconic landmarks such as the Belgrade Fortress (Kalemegdan), which offers panoramic views of the confluence of the Sava and Danube rivers. Wander through the cobblestone streets and discover centuries-old churches, charming cafes, and lively squares.

Dorćol:

Dorćol is one of Belgrade's oldest and most eclectic neighborhoods, known for its bohemian atmosphere and vibrant street life. Explore Skadarlija, Belgrade's answer to Montmartre, with its cobblestone streets, art galleries, and traditional kafanas (taverns). Dorćol is also home to the Jewish Quarter, with its historic synagogue and bustling marketplaces.

Savamala:

Savamala is Belgrade's creative hub, characterized by its industrial-chic vibe and street art scene. Once a neglected area, Savamala has undergone a revitalization in recent years, with abandoned warehouses transformed into art galleries, cafes, and nightclubs. Explore the quirky bars and restaurants along the banks of the Sava River, and don't miss the Belgrade Market Hall, a foodie's paradise.

Vračar:

Vračar is a residential neighborhood known for its leafy streets, elegant architecture, and cultural landmarks. Visit the imposing St. Sava Temple, one of the largest Orthodox churches in the world, and explore the nearby Nikola Tesla Museum, dedicated to the famous Serbian inventor. Vračar is also home to numerous parks and green spaces, perfect for a leisurely stroll or picnic.

Zemun:

Situated on the banks of the Danube River, Zemun is a picturesque neighborhood with a distinct Central European flair. Explore the cobblestone streets of the Old Town, lined with charming cafes, restaurants, and boutiques. Climb the Gardos Tower for panoramic views of the river and city skyline, and don't miss the lively waterfront promenade, ideal for a scenic walk or bike ride.

New Belgrade:

New Belgrade is a modern, bustling neighborhood known for its skyscrapers, shopping malls, and business districts. Explore the sleek architecture of the Belgrade Waterfront, a major urban redevelopment project along the Sava River. Visit the Sava Centar, one of the largest convention centers in Southeast Europe, and enjoy shopping, dining, and entertainment at the Delta City Mall.

Top Attractions
Kalemegdan Fortress:

Perched at the confluence of the Sava and Danube rivers, Kalemegdan Fortress is a symbol of Belgrade's rich past. Originally built by the Romans, the fortress has undergone numerous transformations over the centuries and today serves as a sprawling park with panoramic views of the city and riverbanks.

Skadarlija:

Known as Belgrade's bohemian quarter, Skadarlija is a cobblestone street lined with charming cafes, restaurants, and art galleries. Wander through this colorful neighborhood to soak up its lively atmosphere, enjoy live music, and indulge in traditional Serbian cuisine.

St. Sava Temple:

Dominating the city skyline, the St. Sava Temple is one of the largest Orthodox churches in the world. This magnificent structure, dedicated to Serbia's patron saint, is a masterpiece of Serbian architecture and a must-visit for its grandeur and spiritual significance.

Ada Ciganlija:

Escape the hustle and bustle of the city and head to Ada Ciganlija, Belgrade's beloved recreational island. Here, you can relax on sandy beaches, swim in the lake, rent a bike, or try your hand at various water sports, making it the perfect retreat for outdoor enthusiasts.

Nikola Tesla Museum:

Pay homage to one of Serbia's greatest inventors at the Nikola Tesla Museum. Explore interactive exhibits, original documents, and Tesla's personal belongings, gaining insight into his revolutionary contributions to science and technology.

Republic Square:

At the heart of Belgrade lies Republic Square, a bustling hub surrounded by historic buildings, including the National Museum and the statue of Prince Mihailo on horseback. Take a leisurely stroll, people-watch at a cafe, or admire the impressive architecture that surrounds the square.

Belgrade Zoo:

Located within the grounds of Kalemegdan Fortress, the Belgrade Zoo is home to a diverse array of animals from around the world. Spend an afternoon exploring the zoo's exhibits, which aim to educate visitors about wildlife conservation and preservation efforts.

House of Flowers:

Delve into the life and legacy of Josip Broz Tito, the former president of Yugoslavia, at the House of Flowers. This memorial complex houses Tito's mausoleum and exhibits dedicated to his political career, providing insight into Yugoslavia's socialist era.

Kalemegdan Fortress

History

The origins of Kalemegdan Fortress trace back to the ancient settlement of Singidunum, founded by the Celtic tribe of Scordisci. It served as a strategic military stronghold due to its commanding position overlooking the rivers, enabling its occupants to control key trade routes and defend against invaders.

Throughout its history, Kalemegdan witnessed numerous battles, sieges, and transformations. The Romans conquered Singidunum in the 1st century AD and expanded the fortress, fortifying it with stone walls and towers. During the Byzantine era, the fortress served as a crucial defensive outpost against barbarian incursions.

In the medieval period, Kalemegdan became the seat of Serbian rulers and underwent further fortification. It reached its zenith under the Serbian despot, Stefan Lazarević, in the 15th century, who strengthened its defenses and added imposing towers and gates.

Following the Ottoman conquest of Belgrade in 1521, Kalemegdan underwent significant alterations, with the Turks adding mosques, baths, and other structures within its walls. The fortress remained under Ottoman control for nearly three centuries until Belgrade was liberated by Serbian forces in the 19th century.

Architecture and Layout

The architectural ensemble of Kalemegdan Fortress reflects its diverse cultural heritage, featuring a blend of Roman, Byzantine, Serbian, and Ottoman elements. Its sprawling complex encompasses ramparts, bastions, gates, towers, and inner citadels, each bearing testament to its tumultuous past.

The most iconic structures within Kalemegdan include the imposing Sahat Kula (Clock Tower), Nebojša Tower, and the Gate of Charles VI. Visitors can also explore the remains of medieval churches, Turkish baths, and artillery depots scattered throughout the fortress.

Modern-Day Attractions

Today, Kalemegdan Fortress serves as a sprawling park and cultural hub, offering visitors a tranquil oasis amidst the bustling city. The grounds are adorned with lush greenery, walking paths, and panoramic viewpoints overlooking the rivers and cityscape.

In addition to its historical significance, Kalemegdan hosts several cultural institutions and attractions, including the Military Museum, Belgrade Zoo, and numerous art installations and exhibitions. It's a popular destination for locals and tourists alike, offering a glimpse into Belgrade's past while providing a picturesque setting for leisure and recreation.

Skadarlija

History

Dating back to the 19th century, Skadarlija has a rich history rooted in the city's cultural and artistic heritage. Originally home to Romani immigrants and craftsmen, the neighborhood underwent a transformation in the late 19th and early 20th centuries when it became a gathering place for poets, writers, artists, and musicians. Many renowned Serbian literary figures, such as Đura Jakšić and Tin Ujević, found inspiration within Skadarlija's bohemian ambiance.

Atmosphere

Today, Skadarlija retains its bohemian spirit, with its narrow cobblestone streets lined with charming cafes, traditional Serbian restaurants (known as kafanas), and art galleries. The area buzzes with activity day and night, as locals and visitors flock to its quaint alleyways to savor the atmosphere, enjoy live music performances, and indulge in authentic Serbian cuisine.

Cafes and Restaurants

Skadarlija is renowned for its kafanas, where you can experience the warmth of Serbian hospitality and taste traditional dishes such as cevapi, sarma, and pljeskavica. Many of these establishments have preserved their historic charm, with rustic interiors adorned with vintage decor and walls adorned with photographs and memorabilia from times gone by.

Live Music and Entertainment

Live music is an integral part of the Skadarlija experience. As you wander the streets, you'll encounter talented musicians serenading patrons with traditional Serbian folk music (known as tamburitza) or jazz melodies, creating an immersive and unforgettable ambiance.

Art and Culture

Skadarlija's artistic legacy is celebrated through its numerous art galleries, showcasing the works of local and international artists. From contemporary paintings to traditional handicrafts, these galleries offer a glimpse into Serbia's vibrant art scene and provide the perfect opportunity to take home a piece of Belgrade's creative spirit.

Exploring Skadarlija

Exploring Skadarlija is a delight in itself. Take a leisurely stroll along its picturesque streets, soak up the vibrant colors and sounds, and immerse yourself in the bohemian atmosphere that has enchanted visitors for generations.

St. Sava Temple

History and Architecture:

Construction of the St. Sava Temple began in 1935, although the church has yet to be fully completed.

The cathedral's design draws inspiration from the architectural style of the medieval Serbian monasteries, particularly the Studenica and Gračanica monasteries.

The central dome, reaching a height of over 70 meters, dominates the skyline of Belgrade, making it a prominent feature of the city's landscape.

The interior of the church is adorned with intricate mosaics, frescoes, and marble elements, showcasing the rich artistic heritage of Serbia.

Significance:

The St. Sava Temple holds immense religious and cultural significance for the Serbian people, serving as a symbol of national identity and pride.

It is a place of worship and pilgrimage for Orthodox Christians from Serbia and beyond, attracting visitors seeking spiritual solace and reflection.

The temple also serves as a venue for various religious ceremonies, including baptisms, weddings, and religious holidays, further cementing its central role in the religious life of Belgrade.

Visiting the St. Sava Temple:

The cathedral is open to visitors throughout the year, offering guided tours and educational programs for those interested in learning more about its history and architecture.

Visitors can explore the interior of the church, marveling at its ornate decorations and religious artworks, as well as enjoy panoramic views of Belgrade from the church's observation deck.

Surrounding the St. Sava Temple is the St. Sava Plateau, a spacious square adorned with fountains, gardens, and monuments, providing a tranquil setting for relaxation and contemplation.

Cultural Events and Activities:

The St. Sava Temple serves as a venue for various cultural events, including concerts, art exhibitions, and religious festivals, which celebrate Serbian heritage and foster community spirit.

Visitors can attend religious services, liturgies, and choir performances, immersing themselves in the rich traditions of Serbian Orthodox worship.

Ada Ciganlija

1. History and Transformation:

Originally a river island, Ada Ciganlija underwent significant transformation in the mid-20th century when it was connected to the mainland, forming a peninsula.

Historically, Ada Ciganlija served as a popular getaway spot for locals, but its full potential as a recreational area was realized in the latter half of the 20th century.

2. Outdoor Activities:

Swimming: Ada boasts several artificial beaches along its shores, making it a favorite destination for sunbathing and swimming during the summer months.

Water Sports: Visitors can indulge in a variety of water sports, including kayaking, paddleboarding, windsurfing, and sailing.

Cycling and Rollerblading: The island features numerous bike and rollerblade paths, offering a scenic route for outdoor enthusiasts to explore the lush surroundings.

Sports Facilities: Ada Ciganlija is equipped with sports fields for football, volleyball, basketball, and tennis, providing ample opportunities for active recreation.

3. Nature and Wildlife:

Ada Ciganlija is a haven for nature lovers, boasting dense forests, meadows, and abundant wildlife.

The island's diverse ecosystem supports a variety of bird species, making it a popular destination for birdwatching enthusiasts.

4. Dining and Entertainment:

Restaurants and Cafes: Ada offers a range of dining options, from waterfront cafes serving Serbian specialties to international cuisine.

Nightlife: As the sun sets, Ada Ciganlija transforms into a vibrant nightlife hub, with bars and clubs lining its shores, offering live music and DJ performances.

5. Family-Friendly Attractions:

Children's Playgrounds: Ada features several playgrounds and recreational areas for kids, making it an ideal destination for families.

Miniature Golf: Families can enjoy a round of miniature golf amidst the island's scenic surroundings.

6. Events and Festivals:

Throughout the year, Ada Ciganlija hosts a variety of events and festivals, including music concerts, sports competitions, and cultural celebrations.

7. Practical Information:

Access: Ada Ciganlija is easily accessible from central Belgrade via public transportation, car, or bicycle.

Facilities: The island is equipped with amenities such as restrooms, changing rooms, and rental services for sports equipment.

Museums and Galleries
National Museum of Serbia:

Located in the heart of Belgrade, this museum is home to an extensive collection of Serbian cultural treasures, spanning from prehistoric times to the modern era. Explore exhibits showcasing archaeology, fine arts, and applied arts, offering insight into Serbia's rich history and artistic heritage.

Belgrade City Museum:

Housed in the historic Old Palace, the Belgrade City Museum offers a fascinating journey through the city's past. Discover exhibitions on Belgrade's urban development, prominent figures, and key historical events, providing valuable context for understanding the capital's evolution over the centuries.

Nikola Tesla Museum:

Dedicated to the life and work of the renowned Serbian-American inventor, Nikola Tesla, this museum offers a unique glimpse into the world of science and innovation. Explore Tesla's original documents, inventions, and experiments, providing insight into his groundbreaking contributions to technology.

Museum of Contemporary Art:

Situated on the banks of the Sava River, this modernist masterpiece houses a vast collection of contemporary artworks from Serbia and beyond. Explore rotating exhibitions featuring painting, sculpture, video art, and multimedia installations, showcasing the diversity and creativity of the contemporary art world.

Military Museum:

Delve into Serbia's military history at this comprehensive museum, located within the historic Belgrade Fortress. From ancient weaponry to modern military technology, the museum's exhibits offer a fascinating overview of Serbia's military achievements, conflicts, and strategic importance throughout the ages.

Gallery of Frescoes:

Nestled within the Church of St. Archangel Michael in Belgrade's historic Zemun neighborhood, this gallery showcases a stunning collection of medieval frescoes. Admire meticulously preserved frescoes dating back to the 16th century, providing insight into Serbia's religious and artistic traditions.

Museum of Yugoslav History:

Explore the legacy of Yugoslavia at this museum complex, which includes the House of Flowers mausoleum, dedicated to Josip Broz Tito, the former leader of Yugoslavia. Discover exhibitions on Yugoslavia's socialist past, Tito's life and leadership, and the country's role in shaping modern Balkan history.

Parks and Gardens
Kalemegdan Park:

Situated at the confluence of the Sava and Danube rivers, Kalemegdan Park is not only Belgrade's largest park but also one of its most iconic landmarks. Home to the historic Kalemegdan Fortress, this sprawling green oasis offers panoramic views of the rivers and the city skyline. Visitors can stroll along tree-lined pathways, admire sculptures and monuments, or simply relax on grassy lawns while taking in the breathtaking scenery.

Tašmajdan Park:

Tašmajdan Park is a popular gathering spot for locals and tourists alike. This charming green space features manicured gardens, shady trees, and a tranquil ambiance, making it the perfect place for a leisurely stroll or a picnic with family and friends. Tašmajdan Park is also home to the Church of St. Mark, an architectural gem with a rich history dating back to the 19th century.

Ada Ciganlija:

Often referred to as "Belgrade's Sea," Ada Ciganlija is a sprawling river island turned recreational paradise. This vibrant outdoor complex boasts lush forests, sandy beaches, and crystal-clear waters, making it a favorite destination for swimming, sunbathing, and water sports during the summer months. Ada Ciganlija also features walking and cycling trails, sports facilities, and numerous cafes and restaurants, ensuring there's something for everyone to enjoy.

Topčider Park:

Tucked away in the peaceful suburb of Topčider, Topčider Park is a verdant oasis beloved for its natural beauty and historical significance. Originally a royal estate dating back to the 19th century, this enchanting park features meandering pathways, scenic ponds, and centuries-old trees. Visitors can explore the park's picturesque landscapes, visit the iconic Topčider Palace, or simply unwind amidst nature's tranquility.

Botanical Garden "Jevremovac":

Located within the grounds of the University of Belgrade, the Botanical Garden "Jevremovac" is a hidden gem waiting to be discovered. Established in the 19th century, this botanical oasis is home to a diverse collection of plant species from around the world, including rare and endangered specimens. Visitors can wander through themed gardens, admire colorful blooms, and learn about the importance of biodiversity and conservation.

CHAPTER 4: Eating and Drinking in Belgrade

Traditional Serbian Cuisine

1. Kalemegdan Park

Arguably the most iconic park in Belgrade, Kalemegdan Park is located at the confluence of the Sava and Danube rivers, adjacent to the historic Kalemegdan Fortress. This sprawling park offers stunning views of the rivers and the city skyline, making it a favorite spot for locals and tourists alike. Visitors can explore winding pathways, verdant gardens, and hidden nooks while admiring historical monuments and sculptures scattered throughout the park. Kalemegdan Park also hosts various cultural events, outdoor concerts, and festivals, adding to its allure as a vibrant public space.

2. Ada Ciganlija

Known as Belgrade's "summer oasis," Ada Ciganlija is a river island turned peninsula located on the Sava River. This expansive recreational area is beloved by locals for its sandy beaches, lush forests, and extensive sports and leisure facilities. Visitors can enjoy swimming, sunbathing, and water sports during the summer months, while the park's cycling and jogging trails attract outdoor enthusiasts year-round. Ada Ciganlija also offers numerous cafes, restaurants, and beach bars, making it a popular destination for relaxation and socializing.

3. Tasmajdan Park

Situated in the heart of Belgrade, Tasmajdan Park is a picturesque green space beloved for its tranquil atmosphere and historical significance. The park is home to the Church of St. Mark, a stunning Serbian Orthodox church known for its intricate frescoes and ornate architecture. Visitors can stroll along tree-lined pathways, admire colorful flower beds, and relax on shaded benches while enjoying views of the surrounding landmarks. Tasmajdan Park also features playgrounds for children, making it a family-friendly destination in the city center.

4. Topcider Park

Topcider Park is a serene oasis renowned for its natural beauty and historical landmarks. The park is home to the Topcider Palace, a former royal residence surrounded by manicured gardens, tranquil ponds, and majestic trees. Visitors can explore winding trails, picnic in scenic meadows, and marvel at the park's diverse flora and fauna. Topcider Park also offers recreational activities such as horseback riding and boating, making it a popular destination for outdoor enthusiasts seeking a peaceful escape from the city.

5. Botanical Garden "Jevremovac"

For those with a passion for botany, the Botanical Garden "Jevremovac" offers a fascinating glimpse into Serbia's rich plant diversity. Located within the University of Belgrade's Faculty of Biology, this historic garden is home to over 2,500 plant species from around the world. Visitors can wander through themed gardens, including medicinal plants, aromatic herbs, and exotic succulents, while learning about the importance of biodiversity and conservation. The Botanical Garden also hosts educational programs, workshops, and guided tours, making it an educational and immersive experience for visitors of all ages.

Popular Restaurants and Cafes

1. Question Mark (Znak pitanja)

Located in the heart of the city, Question Mark is one of Belgrade's oldest and most iconic restaurants. Housed in a historic building dating back to 1823, this charming establishment serves up traditional Serbian dishes in a cozy and inviting atmosphere. Be sure to try their famous pljeskavica (grilled meat patty) or sarma (cabbage rolls) for a truly authentic taste of Serbian cuisine.

2. Ambar

For a modern take on traditional Serbian food, head to Ambar in the trendy neighborhood of Beton Hala. This stylish restaurant offers a unique dining experience with its innovative small plates menu, featuring dishes like ajvar (roasted red pepper spread), ćevapi (grilled minced meat), and rakija (fruit brandy). The riverside location offers stunning views of the Sava River, making it the perfect spot for a leisurely meal with friends.

3. Salon 5

Salon 5 is a hidden gem known for its creative cuisine and elegant ambiance. This upscale restaurant showcases the best of Serbian and international flavors, with dishes like roasted lamb with truffle risotto and homemade pasta with wild mushrooms. Pair your meal with a bottle of fine Serbian wine for the ultimate dining experience.

4. Manufaktura

If you're craving comfort food with a modern twist, look no further than Manufaktura. This cozy bistro, located in the bohemian quarter of Skadarlija, serves up hearty dishes made from locally sourced ingredients. From juicy burgers and crispy fried chicken to indulgent desserts like apple strudel and chocolate fondant, Manufaktura has something to satisfy every craving.

5. Kafeterija

For coffee lovers, Kafeterija is a must-visit destination in Belgrade. With several locations across the city, this specialty coffee chain is renowned for its expertly roasted beans and artisanal brews. Whether you prefer a classic espresso or a creamy latte, you'll find the perfect cup of coffee to fuel your day of exploring the city.

6. Coffee Dream

Another beloved coffee spot in Belgrade is Coffee Dream, a cozy cafe chain known for its welcoming atmosphere and delicious pastries. Treat yourself to a slice of homemade cake or indulge in a decadent chocolate croissant while sipping on a freshly brewed cup of coffee. With its relaxed vibe and friendly staff, Coffee Dream is the perfect place to unwind and recharge.

7. Dijagonala 2.0

For a taste of contemporary Serbian cuisine, head to Dijagonala 2.0 in the bustling Savamala district. This sleek and stylish restaurant offers a creative menu featuring dishes inspired by traditional Serbian flavors, with a modern twist.

From delicate seafood ceviche to tender beef tenderloin with truffle sauce, every dish at Dijagonala 2.0 is a work of art.

8. Manufaktura Kafana

For an authentic Serbian dining experience, make your way to Manufaktura Kafana in the heart of Skadarlija. This traditional tavern is famous for its hearty Serbian dishes, live music, and lively atmosphere. Enjoy classics like pljeskavica, ćevapi, and gibanica (cheese pie) while soaking up the bohemian charm of Belgrade's historic cobblestone streets.

9. Smokvica

With its chic decor and laid-back vibe, Smokvica is a favorite hangout spot for locals and expats alike. This trendy cafe offers a diverse menu featuring fresh salads, gourmet sandwiches, and homemade pastries, as well as a selection of craft cocktails and fine wines. Whether you're stopping by for brunch, lunch, or dinner, Smokvica is sure to impress with its delicious food and stylish ambiance.

10. Homa Bistrot

Situated in the leafy Vračar neighborhood, Homa Bistrot is a charming bistro known for its seasonal menu and farm-to-table ethos. This cozy restaurant sources its ingredients from local farmers and producers, ensuring that every dish is bursting with flavor and freshness. From delicate salads and homemade soups to hearty mains and decadent desserts, Homa Bistrot offers a taste of Serbian hospitality at its finest.

Street Food
1. Ćevapi

A staple of Serbian cuisine, Ćevapi are small grilled sausages made from a mixture of minced meat (usually a combination of beef, pork, and lamb), garlic, and various spices. Served hot off the grill and nestled in a fluffy somun (flatbread), Ćevapi are typically accompanied by diced onions and a dollop of ajvar, a flavorful roasted red pepper and eggplant spread. These delicious morsels are ubiquitous in Belgrade, with numerous street vendors and fast-food joints offering their own take on this beloved dish.

2. Pljeskavica

Often referred to as the Serbian hamburger, Pljeskavica is a grilled meat patty made from a mixture of minced beef, pork, and lamb. Seasoned with onions, garlic, and an array of spices, the patty is grilled to perfection and served in a fluffy somun or lepinja (flatbread) with a variety of toppings such as kajmak (a creamy dairy spread), ajvar, lettuce, tomato, and onions. A quintessential street food item, Pljeskavica is a hearty and satisfying meal that embodies the essence of Serbian comfort food.

3. Burek

Originating from the Balkans, Burek is a savory pastry made from thin layers of flaky phyllo dough filled with a variety of ingredients, most commonly minced meat, cheese, or spinach. In Belgrade, Burek is a beloved street food snack that can be enjoyed any time of day, whether as a quick breakfast on the go or a late-night indulgence after a night out. Served piping hot and freshly baked, Burek is best enjoyed with a dollop of yogurt or sour cream on the side.

4. Đuveč

A hearty and comforting dish, Đuveč is a type of vegetable stew made with an assortment of seasonal vegetables, such as tomatoes, peppers, zucchini, eggplant, and potatoes, cooked together with rice or bulgur wheat and flavored with aromatic herbs and spices. Often prepared in large batches and served from street food stalls or food trucks, Đuveč is a popular choice among locals and visitors alike, offering a wholesome and flavorful meal that's perfect for warming up on a chilly day.

5. Palačinke

No exploration of Belgrade's street food scene would be complete without indulging in Palačinke, thin and delicate crepes that are a favorite sweet treat among locals. Served with an array of fillings and toppings, including Nutella, jam, fresh fruit, whipped cream, and even savory options like cheese or ham, Palačinke are a versatile and customizable snack that's perfect for satisfying your sweet tooth on the go.

6. Roasted Chestnuts

As the weather turns cooler, the streets of Belgrade come alive with the irresistible aroma of Roasted Chestnuts. Sold by street vendors in paper cones, these warm and toasty treats are a beloved seasonal snack that's synonymous with autumn and winter in the city. Whether you're strolling along Knez Mihailova Street or exploring the bustling markets of Dorćol, be sure to keep an eye out for these delicious chestnuts, which offer a comforting and nostalgic taste of Belgrade's street food culture.

Nightlife
1. Clubbing Culture:

Belgrade boasts an eclectic and diverse clubbing scene, with venues ranging from underground techno clubs to glamorous rooftop bars. One of the city's most famous nightlife districts is Savamala, where you'll find an array of clubs housed in industrial buildings and warehouses. Popular clubs include Drugstore, 20/44, and KC Grad, known for their cutting-edge music and lively crowds.

2. Floating River Clubs (Splavovi):

A quintessential part of Belgrade's nightlife is its floating river clubs, known locally as "splavovi." Moored along the banks of the Sava and Danube rivers, these floating venues offer a unique party experience with stunning river views and a lively atmosphere. Some of the most popular splavovi include Splav Play, Freestyler, and Lasta, where you can dance the night away to the latest beats spun by top DJs.

3. Bohemian Quarter of Skadarlija:

For a more laid-back and traditional nightlife experience, head to Skadarlija, Belgrade's charming bohemian quarter. Lined with cobblestone streets and quaint cafes, Skadarlija comes alive at night with live music performances, traditional Serbian cuisine, and a relaxed ambiance. Enjoy a leisurely dinner accompanied by live folk music, followed by drinks at one of the many cozy bars scattered throughout the area.

4. Knez Mihailova Street:

As one of the city's main pedestrian thoroughfares, Knez Mihailova Street is not only a shopper's paradise but also a hub for nightlife enthusiasts. Lined with chic cafes, trendy bars, and stylish lounges, this bustling street offers a lively atmosphere well into the early hours of the morning. Join the fashionable crowd for cocktails and people-watching at one of the street's trendy establishments.

5. Underground Scene:

Belgrade's underground music scene is thriving, with a plethora of alternative venues and events catering to electronic music lovers and subculture enthusiasts. From intimate basement clubs to DIY warehouse parties, the city's underground scene offers a raw and authentic experience for those seeking something off the beaten path. Keep an eye out for pop-up events and secret parties advertised through word of mouth and social media channels.

6. Late-Night Eats:

No night out in Belgrade is complete without indulging in some late-night eats. Fortunately, the city boasts a plethora of 24-hour bakeries, street food vendors, and kebab shops serving up delicious snacks and hearty meals well into the early hours. Whether you're craving a greasy burek or a savory pljeskavica, you'll find plenty of options to satisfy your hunger after a long night of partying.

CHAPTER 5: Shopping in Belgrade

Markets and Bazaars

1. Kalenić Market (Kalenićeva pijaca):

Located in the heart of the Vračar neighborhood, Kalenić Market is one of Belgrade's oldest and largest open-air markets. Here, you'll find an abundance of fresh fruits and vegetables, locally sourced meats and cheeses, homemade pastries, and more. The market is a favorite among locals for its quality produce and lively atmosphere. Don't miss the chance to sample some traditional Serbian delicacies and engage in friendly banter with the vendors.

2. Zeleni Venac Market:

Situated near the city center, Zeleni Venac Market is a bustling marketplace known for its diverse selection of goods. From fresh flowers and spices to clothing and household items, this market offers a little bit of everything. Be sure to explore the indoor section of the market, where you'll find an array of local specialties, including cured meats, cheeses, and pickled vegetables. Zeleni Venac Market is a great place to experience the sights, sounds, and flavors of everyday life in Belgrade.

3. Bajloni Market (Bajlonijeva pijaca):

Tucked away in the historic Dorćol neighborhood, Bajloni Market exudes old-world charm and character. This quaint market is known for its artisanal food products, including homemade jams, honey, olive oil, and cured meats. In addition to food items, Bajloni Market also features a flea market section where you can hunt for unique antiques, vintage clothing, and collectibles. Take your time strolling through the market's narrow aisles, soaking in the ambiance and mingling with the locals.

4. Skadarlija Bazaar:

Skadarlija, often referred to as Belgrade's "bohemian quarter," is home to a charming bazaar where you can find a treasure trove of souvenirs, handicrafts, and artisanal goods. The narrow cobblestone streets are lined with colorful stalls selling everything from handmade jewelry and ceramics to traditional Serbian instruments and textiles. After browsing the stalls, be sure to stop at one of the nearby cafes or restaurants to enjoy a leisurely meal and soak up the bohemian atmosphere of Skadarlija.

5. Buvljak Flea Market:

For those in search of vintage treasures and unique finds, Buvljak Flea Market is a must-visit destination. Located on the outskirts of Belgrade, this sprawling market is a paradise for bargain hunters and collectors. Here, you'll find a vast array of secondhand goods, including clothing, furniture, electronics, books, and more. The market is a melting pot of cultures and traditions, with vendors from all walks of life selling their wares. Whether you're on the hunt for a rare vinyl record or a quirky piece of retro furniture, Buvljak Flea Market is sure to delight the discerning shopper.

Shopping Districts
1. Knez Mihailova Street (Knez)

Knez Mihailova Street, often referred to as Knez, is Belgrade's premier shopping destination and one of the oldest and most picturesque streets in the city. Lined with elegant buildings, charming cafes, and a variety of shops, Knez Mihailova Street offers a mix of high-end fashion boutiques, international brands, souvenir shops, and local artisans selling handmade crafts. It's the perfect place to indulge in some retail therapy while soaking up the vibrant atmosphere of Belgrade's bustling city center.

2. Terazije and Kralja Milana Street

Adjacent to Knez Mihailova Street, Terazije Square and Kralja Milana Street form another bustling shopping district in central Belgrade. Here, you'll find a mix of department stores, designer boutiques, and specialty shops offering everything from fashion and accessories to electronics and home goods. Terazije Center, one of the city's oldest shopping malls, is also located here, providing shoppers with a wide range of shopping and dining options under one roof.

3. Usce Shopping Center

Located on the bank of the Sava River, Usce Shopping Center is one of Belgrade's largest and most modern shopping malls. With over 140 stores, including international brands, fashion retailers, and entertainment venues, Usce offers a comprehensive shopping experience for visitors of all ages. In addition to its diverse range of shops, the mall features a food court, cinema complex, and recreational facilities, making it a popular destination for both locals and tourists alike.

4. Delta City

Situated in the New Belgrade district, Delta City is another major shopping destination in the city. Boasting over 200 stores, including fashion brands, electronics retailers, and entertainment options, Delta City caters to the needs of shoppers looking for the latest trends and products. The mall also features a wide range of dining options, as well as a multiplex cinema and children's play area, making it a popular choice for families and leisure seekers.

5. Bajloni Market (Bajlonijeva pijaca)

For a taste of authentic Belgrade shopping, head to Bajloni Market in the Vracar district. This bustling open-air market offers a vibrant mix of fresh produce, local delicacies, clothing, accessories, and household goods. With its lively atmosphere and friendly vendors, Bajloni Market provides visitors with a unique shopping experience and a glimpse into everyday life in Belgrade. Don't forget to haggle for the best deals and sample some of the delicious street food on offer!

6. Zeleni Venac Market

Zeleni Venac Market, located near the city center, is one of Belgrade's oldest and most iconic markets. Here, you'll find a wide variety of fresh fruits, vegetables, meats, cheeses, and other culinary delights, sourced directly from local producers. In addition to its food offerings, Zeleni Venac Market also features stalls selling flowers, clothing, and household goods, making it a popular spot for both shopping and socializing.

Souvenirs and Gifts
Traditional Handicrafts:

One of the best ways to experience Serbian culture is through its traditional handicrafts. From intricately woven rugs and embroidered textiles to hand-painted ceramics and wooden carvings, Belgrade's markets and artisan shops are filled with exquisite examples of local craftsmanship.

Rakija:

No visit to Serbia is complete without sampling rakija, the country's beloved fruit brandy. Made from a variety of fruits such as plum, apricot, and quince, rakija is a staple in Serbian culture and makes for a memorable souvenir. You can find bottles of rakija in various flavors and sizes at local markets and specialty liquor stores throughout Belgrade.

Ajvar:

A staple of Serbian cuisine, ajvar is a savory red pepper relish that's bursting with flavor. Made from roasted peppers, garlic, and chili peppers, ajvar is a versatile condiment that pairs perfectly with bread, cheese, and grilled meats. Pick up a jar of ajvar from a local market or grocery store to enjoy a taste of Serbia at home.

Handcrafted Jewelry:

Serbian jewelry artisans are known for their intricate designs and attention to detail. Whether you're drawn to traditional filigree pieces or contemporary designs inspired by Serbian folklore, you'll find a stunning selection of handcrafted jewelry in Belgrade's boutiques and artisan markets.

Orthodox Icons:

Serbia's rich religious heritage is reflected in its beautifully crafted Orthodox icons. These religious paintings, often adorned with gold leaf and intricate details, are not only objects of devotion but also works of art. You can find a wide range of Orthodox icons depicting saints, biblical scenes, and religious motifs at souvenir shops and religious stores across Belgrade.

Traditional Costumes:

Immerse yourself in Serbian culture by donning a traditional costume, complete with embroidered vests, colorful skirts, and ornate headdresses. Whether you're attending a folk festival or simply want to channel your inner Serbian spirit, traditional costumes make for a unique and memorable souvenir.

Films and Music:

Bring home a piece of Serbian entertainment by purchasing DVDs of classic Serbian films or albums by local musicians. From traditional folk music to contemporary pop and rock, Serbia has a rich musical heritage that's worth exploring.

Artisanal Foods:

Stock up on artisanal foods and gourmet treats to enjoy a taste of Serbia long after your trip is over. From organic honey and homemade jams to cured meats and artisanal cheeses, Belgrade's markets are a food lover's paradise.

CHAPTER 6: Day Trips from Belgrade

Novi Sad

1. Discovering Novi Sad's History

Novi Sad boasts a long and storied history that dates back to ancient times. The city's roots can be traced to the Roman era, and evidence of its past can still be seen in its well-preserved architecture and archaeological sites. One of the most iconic landmarks is the Petrovaradin Fortress, a massive fortress perched atop a hill overlooking the Danube. Built in the 18th century, the fortress offers panoramic views of the city and hosts numerous cultural events, including the famous EXIT music festival.

2. Exploring Novi Sad's Cultural Scene

Novi Sad is often referred to as the cultural capital of Serbia, and for good reason. The city is home to a thriving arts and music scene, with numerous galleries, theaters, and music venues scattered throughout its streets. Visitors can explore the Museum of Vojvodina to learn about the region's history and heritage, or catch a performance at the Serbian National Theatre, which showcases a variety of theatrical productions, opera, and ballet.

3. Sampling Novi Sad's Culinary Delights

No visit to Novi Sad would be complete without indulging in the city's culinary delights. From traditional Serbian cuisine to international fare, Novi Sad offers a diverse array of dining options to suit every palate. Be sure to sample local specialties such as Ćevapi (grilled minced meat), sarma (cabbage rolls), and ajvar (a savory pepper spread). For a taste of the city's vibrant cafe culture, head to Dunavska Street, where you can relax and unwind with a cup of coffee while soaking in the charming atmosphere.

4. Getting Active in Novi Sad's Great Outdoors

For outdoor enthusiasts, Novi Sad offers plenty of opportunities for adventure and exploration. The nearby Fruška Gora National Park is a haven for hikers and nature lovers, boasting lush forests, scenic trails, and hidden monasteries tucked away in the hills. Visitors can also enjoy boating, fishing, and picnicking along the banks of the Danube, or take a leisurely bike ride along the city's picturesque waterfront promenade.

5. Immersing Yourself in Novi Sad's Festivals and Events

Throughout the year, Novi Sad plays host to a variety of festivals and events that celebrate its rich cultural heritage and artistic spirit. The most famous of these is the EXIT music festival, one of the largest and most popular music festivals in Europe. Held annually at the Petrovaradin Fortress, EXIT attracts thousands of music lovers from around the world who come to enjoy performances by top international artists across a range of genres.

Sremski Karlovci
History and Heritage

Sremski Karlovci traces its roots back to the Roman era when it served as an important military outpost and trading center. However, it wasn't until the 18th century that the town flourished, becoming a cultural and educational hub for the Serbian people under Habsburg rule.

One of the town's most significant historical moments occurred in 1699 when the Treaty of Karlowitz was signed, marking the end of the Great Turkish War and establishing Sremski Karlovci as an important diplomatic center in Europe.

Architectural Treasures

Wandering through the streets of Sremski Karlovci feels like stepping back in time. The town is dotted with beautifully preserved buildings, churches, and monuments that showcase its rich architectural heritage.

One of the most iconic landmarks in Sremski Karlovci is the Cathedral of St. Nicholas, a stunning Baroque masterpiece that dominates the town's skyline. Other notable sites include the Patriarchal Residence, the Theological School, and the Chapel of Peace, where the Treaty of Karlowitz was negotiated.

Wine and Gastronomy

Sremski Karlovci is renowned for its wine production, with vineyards dating back centuries. Visitors can explore local wineries, sample a variety of wines, and learn about the winemaking process from knowledgeable vintners.

In addition to its wine culture, Sremski Karlovci offers a variety of culinary delights, including traditional Serbian dishes and regional specialties. Don't miss the opportunity to taste local delicacies such as čvarci (pork cracklings), karađorđeva šnicla (stuffed veal), and krofne (Serbian doughnuts).

Cultural and Educational Institutions

Despite its small size, Sremski Karlovci boasts a rich cultural scene, with several museums, galleries, and libraries showcasing the town's artistic and intellectual heritage. The Matica Srpska Gallery houses a remarkable collection of Serbian art, while the Museum of Beekeeping offers insight into the region's agricultural traditions.

The town is also home to the Seminary Library, one of the oldest and most important libraries in Serbia, containing rare manuscripts, books, and documents dating back centuries.

Outdoor Activities

Surrounded by the stunning landscapes of the Fruška Gora National Park, Sremski Karlovci offers ample opportunities for outdoor recreation and exploration. Visitors can hike through scenic trails, picnic in lush forests, or simply soak in the natural beauty of the countryside.

For those interested in adventure sports, the nearby Danube River provides opportunities for kayaking, canoeing, and fishing, while the surrounding hills are ideal for cycling and horseback riding.

Vojvodina

Geography and Landscape:

Vojvodina is characterized by its flat terrain, punctuated by fertile plains, rivers, and low hills. The region is primarily situated in the Pannonian Basin, making it an important agricultural area known for its vast fields of wheat, corn, and sunflowers. The Danube River runs along Vojvodina's northern border, offering picturesque landscapes and opportunities for river cruises.

Cultural Diversity:

One of the most striking aspects of Vojvodina is its cultural diversity. The region is home to numerous ethnic groups, including Serbs, Hungarians, Croats, Slovaks, Romanians, and others. This rich tapestry of cultures has contributed to Vojvodina's vibrant atmosphere and is reflected in its architecture, cuisine, and traditions.

Historical Significance:

Vojvodina has a rich history that spans millennia. Throughout the centuries, it has been inhabited by various civilizations, including the Romans, Huns, Byzantines, Ottomans, and Austro-Hungarians. This diverse historical legacy is evident in the region's architecture, with medieval fortresses, Baroque palaces, and charming villages dotting the landscape.

Novi Sad:

Novi Sad is the capital of Vojvodina and its largest city. Known as the "Athens of Serbia" for its cultural significance, Novi Sad is home to numerous museums, galleries, theaters, and festivals. The Petrovaradin Fortress, overlooking the Danube River, is one of the city's most iconic landmarks and hosts the renowned EXIT music festival annually.

Sremski Karlovci:

This picturesque town is famous for its winemaking tradition and historic architecture. Visitors can explore its charming streets lined with Baroque buildings, visit the Orthodox Cathedral of St. Nicholas, and sample local wines at one of the town's many wineries.

Ethnic Enclaves:

Throughout Vojvodina, visitors can discover unique ethnic enclaves that reflect the region's multicultural heritage. From the Hungarian-influenced town of Subotica to the Slovak village of Kovačica, each enclave offers a glimpse into the traditions and customs of its respective community.

Natural Attractions:

Vojvodina is not only rich in cultural heritage but also boasts stunning natural landscapes. The Fruška Gora National Park, located just south of Novi Sad, is a lush forested area with hiking trails, monasteries, and vineyards. Additionally, the Deliblato Sands, a vast sandy area in eastern Vojvodina, is a unique ecosystem perfect for outdoor enthusiasts.

Cuisine:

Vojvodina's culinary scene is a reflection of its cultural diversity. Visitors can indulge in hearty Serbian dishes such as čevapi (grilled meat), sarma (cabbage rolls), and ajvar (roasted red pepper spread), as well as Hungarian specialties like goulash and lángos (fried dough). Don't forget to accompany your meal with a glass of local wine or rakija (fruit brandy) for a truly authentic experience.

Šumadija Region
1. Natural Beauty:

The Šumadija region is blessed with breathtaking natural beauty, characterized by rolling hills, lush forests, and fertile valleys. Visitors can explore the stunning landscapes of the Oplenac area, known for its vineyards and orchards, or venture into the dense woodlands of the Rudnik Mountain, where hiking trails offer panoramic views of the surrounding countryside.

2. Cultural Heritage:

Šumadija is steeped in history and boasts a wealth of cultural heritage sites. One of the region's highlights is the Šumadija Museum in Kragujevac, which showcases the rich history and traditions of the area through its diverse exhibits and artifacts. Additionally, visitors can explore the historic town of Topola, home to the majestic Karadjordjevic Royal Complex, where Serbia's royal dynasty traces its roots.

3. Monasteries and Churches:

Šumadija is dotted with ancient monasteries and churches, offering a glimpse into Serbia's spiritual heritage. The renowned Oplenac Mausoleum, adorned with stunning mosaics depicting Serbian history and culture, is a must-visit attraction in the region. Other notable religious sites include the beautifully preserved monasteries of Vracevsnica and Studenica, each boasting remarkable architecture and serene surroundings.

4. Traditional Villages:

Explore the charming villages of Šumadija, where time seems to stand still. Picturesque hamlets like Risovača and

Drača offer a glimpse into traditional Serbian life, with their quaint houses, cobblestone streets, and warm hospitality. Visitors can immerse themselves in rural customs and traditions, from sampling homemade delicacies to participating in folk festivals and celebrations.

5. Outdoor Activities:

Šumadija is a paradise for outdoor enthusiasts, offering a wide range of recreational activities amidst its stunning natural landscapes. From hiking and biking to horseback riding and fishing, there's no shortage of adventures to be had. Nature lovers can also explore the pristine beauty of the Mlava River Gorge or unwind in the tranquil surroundings of the Divčibare mountain resort.

6. Culinary Delights:

Indulge in the flavors of Šumadija's traditional cuisine, which celebrates the region's bountiful harvests and culinary heritage. Sample hearty dishes like roasted lamb, grilled meats, and savory pies, accompanied by locally produced wines and spirits. Don't miss the opportunity to visit a rural farmstead or tavern, where you can savor authentic farm-to-table cuisine in a rustic setting.

7. Festivals and Events:

Experience the vibrant cultural scene of Šumadija through its colorful festivals and events. From traditional folklore performances to wine tastings and harvest celebrations, there's always something happening in the region. Plan your visit during the annual Šumadija Wine Route Festival or the Kragujevac October Salon, and immerse yourself in the rich tapestry of Šumadija's cultural heritage.

CHAPTER 7: Practical Information

Language and Communication

Serbian Language:

Serbian is the predominant language spoken by the majority of Belgrade's inhabitants. It belongs to the South Slavic branch of the Slavic language family and is written in the Cyrillic script, although the Latin script is also widely used. Visitors to Belgrade will find that many signs, menus, and official documents are written in both scripts, reflecting the country's linguistic duality.

For travelers unfamiliar with the Serbian language, learning a few basic phrases can greatly enhance the overall experience. Common greetings such as "Zdravo" (Hello), "Hvala" (Thank you), and "Doviđenja" (Goodbye) are always appreciated and can go a long way in establishing rapport with locals.

English Language:

English proficiency among the residents of Belgrade varies widely, with younger generations generally more fluent than older generations. In tourist areas, hotels, restaurants, and shops, it's common to find English-speaking staff who can assist visitors with basic inquiries and transactions.

However, outside of these tourist hubs, English proficiency may be limited, particularly among older individuals. In such cases, having a phrasebook or translation app handy can be invaluable for overcoming language barriers and navigating everyday interactions.

Other Languages:

Belgrade's linguistic diversity extends beyond Serbian and English, owing to the city's multicultural heritage. Other languages commonly spoken in Belgrade include:

Hungarian: Belgrade is home to a significant Hungarian minority, particularly in areas such as Vojvodina, where Hungarian is recognized as an official language alongside Serbian.

Romani: The Romani community, also known as the Roma or Gypsy community, has a presence in Belgrade, with Romani being spoken by some members of this community.

Other Minority Languages: Due to Serbia's multicultural makeup, languages such as Albanian, Bosnian, Croatian, and Bulgarian may also be heard in certain neighborhoods, reflecting the city's diverse population.

Communication Tips:

Be Respectful: While many Belgraders are multilingual and accustomed to interacting with visitors from diverse backgrounds, it's essential to approach communication with respect and an open-minded attitude.

Learn Basic Phrases: Even if English is widely spoken, making an effort to learn a few basic phrases in Serbian can demonstrate goodwill and enhance your interactions with locals.

Use Gestures: In situations where language barriers persist, non-verbal communication such as gestures, facial expressions, and body language can help convey meaning and facilitate understanding.

Be Patient: Patience is key when navigating language barriers, especially in situations where communication may be challenging. Take your time, remain calm, and approach interactions with a spirit of understanding and flexibility.

Currency and Money Matters
1. Currency:

The official currency of Serbia is the Serbian Dinar (RSD), abbreviated as "din" or "дин" in Cyrillic script.

The dinar is issued in both coins (dinars) and banknotes (novčanice), with denominations ranging from 1 to 1000 dinars for coins and 10 to 5000 dinars for banknotes.

While some establishments may accept euros (€) or other major currencies, it's advisable to use the local currency for transactions to avoid unfavorable exchange rates.

2. Exchange Rates:

Exchange rates for the Serbian Dinar can fluctuate, so it's recommended to check the latest rates before exchanging your currency.

Exchange offices (menjačnica) are widely available throughout Belgrade, particularly in tourist areas, major transportation hubs, and commercial districts.

It's advisable to compare rates at different exchange offices to ensure you get the best value for your money. Avoid exchanging currency at unofficial or unlicensed establishments.

3. Banking:

Major banks in Belgrade include Raiffeisen Bank, UniCredit Bank, Societe Generale Bank, and Komercijalna Banka, among others. These banks provide a wide range of services, including currency exchange, ATM withdrawals, and international money transfers.

ATMs (bankomat) are prevalent throughout the city, allowing you to withdraw Serbian Dinars using international debit or credit cards. Be aware of potential ATM fees charged by your bank for overseas transactions.

Most banks in Belgrade operate on weekdays from Monday to Friday, with limited hours on Saturdays. Banking hours may vary depending on the specific branch and location.

4. Payment Methods:

Cash is widely accepted in Belgrade, especially for smaller transactions, street vendors, and local markets. It's advisable to carry small denominations of dinars for convenience.

Credit and debit cards are accepted at many hotels, restaurants, shops, and tourist attractions, particularly in more upscale establishments and tourist areas. However, it's always a good idea to carry some cash as a backup, especially in more remote or cash-only establishments.

Contactless payment methods, such as NFC-enabled cards and mobile payment apps, are becoming increasingly popular in Belgrade, offering a convenient and secure way to make transactions.

5. Tipping:

Tipping in Belgrade is not mandatory but is appreciated for good service. In restaurants, a tip of 10% is customary if a service charge is not included in the bill. You can also round up the bill or leave small change for waitstaff.

It's customary to tip taxi drivers by rounding up the fare to the nearest whole amount or adding a small additional tip for excellent service.

Safety Tips

Stay Aware of Your Surroundings:

Be mindful of your surroundings, especially in crowded areas and tourist spots. Keep an eye on your belongings, and be cautious of pickpockets, particularly in busy markets, public transportation, and major attractions.

Use Licensed Taxis:

When taking a taxi, make sure to use licensed ones with clearly displayed taxi signs. Avoid unmarked or unofficial taxis, as they may overcharge or engage in fraudulent practices. It's advisable to ask your accommodation to arrange a taxi for you or use reputable taxi apps.

Avoid Solo Nighttime Walks:

While Belgrade is generally safe at night, it's wise to avoid walking alone in secluded or poorly lit areas, especially after dark. Stick to well-lit streets and busy areas, and consider using transportation or reputable ride-sharing services if you're out late.

Beware of Scams:

Be cautious of scams targeting tourists, such as fake petitions, distraction techniques, or offers that seem too good to be true. Keep your valuables secure, and don't engage with suspicious individuals or unsolicited offers.

Respect Local Laws and Customs:

Familiarize yourself with Serbian laws and customs to avoid any misunderstandings or legal issues. For example, public drinking is prohibited in certain areas, and smoking is banned in indoor public spaces. Additionally, avoid discussing sensitive political topics in public.

Use ATMs Wisely:

When using ATMs, choose machines located in well-lit and secure areas, such as inside banks or shopping malls. Shield your PIN while entering it, and be cautious of anyone loitering nearby. Consider using ATMs during daylight hours or inside secure premises.

Stay Informed About Current Events:

Stay informed about any current events or potential safety concerns in Belgrade by checking local news sources and advisories. Be aware of any demonstrations, protests, or public gatherings that may impact your travel plans, and avoid participating or getting caught in any unrest.

Secure Your Accommodation:

Choose reputable accommodation options with secure locks and safety measures in place. Use hotel safes to store your valuables, and ensure that doors and windows are securely locked, especially when leaving your room unattended.

Emergency Contacts:

Keep a list of emergency contacts handy, including local authorities, your country's embassy or consulate, and your accommodation's contact information. Program important numbers into your phone and carry a physical copy as well.

Trust Your Instincts:

Above all, trust your instincts and use common sense while traveling in Belgrade. If something feels off or uncomfortable, remove yourself from the situation and seek assistance if necessary.

Etiquette and Customs
Greetings and Politeness:

When meeting someone for the first time, a firm handshake and direct eye contact are customary.

Use formal titles and last names until invited to use first names, especially in business settings.

It's polite to greet people with "Dobar dan" (Good day) during the day and "Dobro veče" (Good evening) after dark.

Hospitality:

Serbians are known for their warm hospitality. If invited into someone's home, it's customary to bring a small gift, such as flowers or chocolates, for the host.

Expect to be offered food and drinks generously. Accepting hospitality is seen as a sign of respect.

Dining Etiquette:

When dining out, it's polite to wait for the host or the eldest person at the table to initiate eating.

Keep your hands visible on the table, rather than resting them in your lap, while dining.

Toasting is common during meals. Raise your glass and say "Živeli!" (To life!) before taking a sip.

Respect for Elders:

Serbian culture places a strong emphasis on respect for elders. Address older individuals with proper titles and show deference in conversation.

Body Language:

Avoid excessive gestures or physical contact, especially with people you've just met. Serbians tend to value personal space.

Pointing with your index finger is considered rude. Instead, use an open hand or gesture with your chin.

Religious Customs:

Serbia is predominantly Eastern Orthodox Christian, and religious customs are deeply ingrained in the culture. Respect religious sites and practices, such as covering your head and shoulders when visiting Orthodox churches.

Language and Communication:

Learning a few basic phrases in Serbian, such as "Hvala" (Thank you) and "Molim" (Please), goes a long way in showing respect for the local language and culture.

Serbians appreciate directness in communication, so don't hesitate to express your opinions or ask questions.

Tipping:

Tipping is not mandatory but is appreciated for good service. A tip of around 10% is customary in restaurants if the service charge is not included in the bill.

Socializing and Nightlife:

Belgrade is famous for its vibrant nightlife scene. When socializing in bars or clubs, expect late nights and lively atmospheres.

Dress to impress, especially if you're planning to visit upscale establishments or attending special events.

Public Behavior:

Smoking is still prevalent in Belgrade, but there are restrictions in indoor public spaces. Always ask before lighting up, and be mindful of non-smokers.

Littering and public drunkenness are frowned upon. Respect the cleanliness of public spaces and the peace of residential areas.

CHAPTER 8: Events and Festivals

Belgrade Beer Fest

History and Evolution

The origins of Belgrade Beer Fest trace back to 2003 when a group of beer enthusiasts had a vision to create a festival that would showcase the rich diversity of Serbian and international beers while celebrating the cultural heritage of Belgrade. What started as a modest gathering has since evolved into a grand extravaganza, drawing in over half a million attendees annually.

Location and Setting

The festival takes place in Usce Park, a sprawling green oasis nestled between the Sava and Danube rivers, offering a picturesque backdrop for the festivities. The park's lush surroundings provide the perfect setting for beer enthusiasts to gather, socialize, and immerse themselves in the vibrant atmosphere.

Brewery Lineup

One of the highlights of Belgrade Beer Fest is its impressive lineup of breweries, featuring both local Serbian breweries and renowned international brands. Visitors have the opportunity to sample a wide array of beers, from traditional Serbian lagers and ales to craft brews and specialty imports from around the world. With countless options to choose from, there's something to satisfy every palate and preference.

Cultural Program

In addition to its stellar beer selection, Belgrade Beer Fest offers a diverse cultural program that showcases the best of Serbian music, art, and entertainment. Live performances by local and international artists grace multiple stages throughout the festival, spanning various genres from rock and pop to folk and electronic music. From traditional folk dances to contemporary art installations, there's no shortage of cultural delights to enjoy amidst the beer-fueled revelry.

Food and Cuisine

No beer festival would be complete without delicious food to complement the brews, and Belgrade Beer Fest delivers on this front as well. A tantalizing array of food stalls and vendors offer a mouthwatering selection of Serbian delicacies, street food favorites, and international cuisines. Whether you're craving hearty pljeskavica (Serbian burger), savory cevapi (grilled sausages), or indulgent street desserts, you'll find plenty of options to satisfy your cravings.

Community and Atmosphere

Beyond the beer and entertainment, Belgrade Beer Fest fosters a sense of community and camaraderie among attendees. From seasoned beer connoisseurs to curious first-timers, festival-goers come together to share in the joy of good beer, great music, and unforgettable experiences. The lively atmosphere is infectious, with laughter, cheers, and the sound of clinking glasses filling the air as strangers become friends amidst the revelry.

Belgrade Music Festival (BEMUS)
History and Evolution

BEMUS traces its roots back to the visionary efforts of prominent Serbian conductor and composer Mladen Jagušt. Under his leadership, the festival was conceived as a platform to celebrate classical music and promote cultural exchange between local and international artists. Over the years, BEMUS has evolved into a globally recognized event, attracting world-renowned musicians, orchestras, and composers to the stages of Belgrade.

Program Highlights

Each year, BEMUS presents an eclectic program featuring a wide range of musical genres and styles. From symphonic masterpieces to experimental works, the festival strives to cater to diverse tastes and interests within the realm of classical and contemporary music. Concerts, recitals, chamber music performances, and multimedia presentations are just a few of the formats showcased throughout the festival's duration.

Venues

BEMUS takes advantage of Belgrade's rich cultural landscape by utilizing a variety of iconic venues across the city. From historic theaters and concert halls to contemporary performance spaces and outdoor stages, the festival transforms Belgrade into a vibrant hub of musical activity. Locations such as the Belgrade Philharmonic Hall, Sava Center, Kolarac Concert Hall, and various churches and galleries serve as the backdrop for BEMUS's diverse program offerings.

International Collaboration

One of the defining features of BEMUS is its commitment to fostering international collaboration and cultural exchange. The festival regularly welcomes acclaimed artists and ensembles from around the world, offering audiences in Belgrade the opportunity to experience performances of the highest caliber. Additionally, BEMUS often partners with cultural institutions, embassies, and music festivals from other countries to curate collaborative projects and showcase the best of global musical talent.

Educational and Outreach Initiatives

In addition to its concert series, BEMUS is dedicated to educational outreach and community engagement. The festival organizes workshops, masterclasses, and lectures aimed at nurturing the next generation of musicians and fostering a deeper appreciation for classical music among audiences of all ages. Through these initiatives, BEMUS continues to uphold its mission of promoting cultural enrichment and artistic excellence in Belgrade and beyond.

EXIT Festival
History and Origins

The roots of the EXIT Festival trace back to the political unrest in Serbia during the late 1990s. As the country struggled under the weight of authoritarian rule, a group of university students in Novi Sad saw the need to organize a festival that would serve as a platform for social change and youth activism. Thus, EXIT was born, with its inaugural edition held in 2000 at the Petrovaradin Fortress, a historic landmark overlooking the Danube River.

Evolution and Growth

Over the years, EXIT has grown exponentially, both in scale and scope. What began as a protest against political oppression has blossomed into a multi-day extravaganza featuring some of the biggest names in music, spanning a diverse range of genres including rock, electronic, hip-hop, reggae, and more. The festival's lineup boasts an impressive roster of international and local artists, with past headliners including The Prodigy, The Killers, Arctic Monkeys, David Guetta, and many others.

Unique Setting and Atmosphere

One of the defining features of the EXIT Festival is its breathtaking location within the Petrovaradin Fortress. Spread across multiple stages and venues within the fortress walls, the festival offers attendees a truly immersive experience, with stunning views of the river below and the city of Novi Sad in the distance. The unique blend of historical architecture and cutting-edge music creates an atmosphere unlike any other, making EXIT a must-visit destination for music lovers and cultural enthusiasts alike.

Beyond the Music

While music remains at the heart of the EXIT Festival, the event also incorporates elements of art, activism, and social responsibility. Throughout the festival grounds, attendees can discover art installations, interactive exhibits, and workshops promoting environmental sustainability, human rights, and social justice. Additionally, EXIT is known for its commitment to supporting local communities and charitable causes, with proceeds from ticket sales going towards various initiatives aimed at making a positive impact in the region.

CHAPTER 9: Further Resources

Useful Websites

Official Belgrade Tourism Website –

The official tourism website for Belgrade provides comprehensive information on attractions, events, accommodations, and transportation options in the city. Visitors can also find useful travel tips and recommendations.

Website: www.beograd.rs/en/

TripAdvisor Belgrade - TripAdvisor offers a plethora of traveler reviews, ratings, and recommendations for hotels, restaurants, attractions, and activities in Belgrade. It's an invaluable resource for planning your trip and discovering hidden gems.

Website: www.tripadvisor.com/Tourism-g294472-Belgrade-Vacations.html

Belgrade In Your Pocket - Belgrade In Your Pocket is a comprehensive online city guide featuring insider tips, reviews, and listings for dining, nightlife, shopping, accommodations, and sightseeing in Belgrade.

Website: www.inyourpocket.com/belgrade

Visit Belgrade Blog - This blog offers insightful articles, travel guides, and tips for exploring Belgrade. From local events to off-the-beaten-path attractions, it provides valuable insights for travelers looking to experience the city like a local.

Website: www.visitbelgrade.info/en/blog

Belgrade MyWay - Belgrade MyWay is a handy online resource offering practical information and guides for tourists visiting Belgrade. It covers topics such as transportation, accommodations, dining, shopping, and sightseeing.

Website: www.belgrademyway.com

Serbia Travel - The Serbia Travel website provides information not only on Belgrade but also on other destinations across Serbia. It offers travel guides, tips, and resources for planning your itinerary beyond the capital city.

Website: www.serbia.travel/en

Time Out Belgrade - Time Out Belgrade offers curated recommendations for things to do, places to eat, and events happening in the city. It's a great resource for staying up-to-date on the latest happenings and trends in Belgrade.

Website: www.timeout.com/belgrade

Belgrade Free Walking Tours - Belgrade Free Walking Tours website provides information about free guided walking tours of the city. It's a fantastic way to explore Belgrade's landmarks and learn about its history from knowledgeable local guides.

Website: www.belgradewalkingtours.com

Belgrade Nightlife Guide - For those interested in Belgrade's vibrant nightlife scene, this website offers insights into the best bars, clubs, and live music venues in the city. Stay updated on upcoming events and parties.

Website: www.belgradenightlife.net

Transportation Authority of Belgrade - The Transportation Authority of Belgrade website provides essential information on public transportation services, including buses, trams, trolleybuses, and the Belgrade Metro.

Website: www.gsp.rs

Belgrade Airport - The official website of Belgrade Nikola Tesla Airport offers flight information, airport services, transportation options to and from the airport, and useful travel tips for visitors arriving or departing from Belgrade by air.

Website: www.beg.aero

Belgrade Weather Forecast - Stay informed about the weather conditions in Belgrade by checking the latest forecasts and updates on this website. It provides detailed weather information, including temperature, precipitation, and wind speed.

Website: www.weather.com/weather/today/l/SRBG0055:1:SR

Belgrade City Library - The Belgrade City Library website offers information about library services, events, and resources available to visitors. It's a great resource for book lovers and those interested in Serbian literature and culture.

Website: www.biblioteka.beograd.rs

Belgrade Art Galleries and Museums - Discover the rich cultural heritage of Belgrade by exploring its art galleries and museums. This website provides information about current exhibitions, opening hours, and admission fees.

Website: www.beltouristguide.rs/art-galleries-museums-belgrade

Belgrade City Calendar - Stay updated on events, festivals, concerts, and cultural happenings in Belgrade with this comprehensive city calendar. Plan your visit to coincide with exciting events and celebrations.

Website: www.cityofbelgrade.net/calendar

Belgrade Expat Community - If you're an expatriate or planning to relocate to Belgrade, this website provides resources, forums, and advice for expats living in the city. Connect with fellow expats and access helpful information about life in Belgrade.

Website: www.belgradeexpat.com

Belgrade City Government - The official website of the Belgrade City Government offers information about local government services, city administration, and municipal initiatives. Visitors can find practical information and contacts for various city departments.

Website: www.beograd.rs/en

Belgrade International Film Festival (FEST) - Film enthusiasts can find information about the annual Belgrade International Film Festival (FEST) on this website, including screening schedules, film synopses, and ticketing details.

Website: www.fest.rs

Belgrade Volunteer Opportunities - If you're interested in volunteering or getting involved in community initiatives during your stay in Belgrade, this website offers information about volunteer opportunities, charitable organizations, and community projects.

Website: www.volunteerbelgrade.rs

Belgrade Live Webcams - Experience Belgrade in real-time with live webcams streaming views of iconic landmarks, city squares, and scenic spots. Whether you're planning your visit or missing the city, these webcams offer a virtual glimpse of Belgrade.

Website: www.webcamtaxi.com/en/serbia/belgrade.html

Useful Apps

Moovit:

Moovit is a comprehensive public transportation app that provides real-time information on bus, tram, and trolleybus schedules in Belgrade. It offers route planning, live updates on delays, and step-by-step navigation to help you get around the city efficiently.

Belgrade City Guide:

This app serves as a digital guidebook to Belgrade, offering information on attractions, restaurants, nightlife, and events. It provides offline maps, reviews, and recommendations to help you discover the best of what the city has to offer.

Car:GO: Car:

GO is a popular ride-hailing app in Belgrade, offering convenient and affordable transportation options. You can book rides with licensed taxi drivers, track your driver's location in real-time, and pay securely through the app.

Parking Servis:

For those driving in Belgrade, the Parking Servis app is essential for finding available parking spots, checking parking rates, and paying for parking using your smartphone. It helps alleviate the stress of finding parking in the city center.

Beogradski Sindikat:

This app provides up-to-date information on cultural events, concerts, exhibitions, and festivals happening in Belgrade. You can browse events by date, category, or location, and purchase tickets directly through the app.

Wolt:

Wolt is a food delivery app that partners with a wide range of restaurants and cafes in Belgrade. Whether you're craving traditional Serbian cuisine or international flavors, you can easily order food for delivery to your doorstep with just a few taps.

Belgrade Taxi:

Belgrade Taxi is another reliable taxi-hailing app that allows you to book rides with licensed taxi companies in Belgrade. It offers upfront pricing, multiple payment options, and the ability to rate your driver after the ride.

Belgrade Airport:

If you're flying into or out of Belgrade Nikola Tesla Airport, this app provides essential information on flight schedules, terminal maps, airport services, and ground transportation options. It helps streamline your travel experience.

Yelp:

Yelp is a useful app for discovering and reviewing local businesses in Belgrade, including restaurants, bars, shops, and attractions. You can read user reviews, view photos, and find recommendations based on your preferences and location.

Google Maps:

While not specific to Belgrade, Google Maps remains an indispensable tool for navigation in the city. It offers detailed maps, turn-by-turn directions, and real-time traffic updates to help you navigate the streets of Belgrade with ease.

Conclusion

As we come to the end of the Belgrade Travel Guide, we hope that this resource has served as a valuable companion on your journey through the Serbian capital. Belgrade, with its rich history, vibrant culture, and warm hospitality, is a city that leaves a lasting impression on all who visit.

From the ancient walls of Kalemegdan Fortress to the lively streets of Skadarlija, Belgrade offers a tapestry of experiences waiting to be explored. Whether you've marveled at the magnificent architecture, indulged in the flavors of Serbian cuisine, or danced the night away in one of the city's clubs, we trust that your time in Belgrade has been filled with memorable moments.

But beyond the sights and sounds, it's the spirit of Belgrade – resilient, welcoming, and full of life – that truly captures the essence of this remarkable city. As you bid farewell to Belgrade, we hope that you carry with you fond memories and a newfound appreciation for this gem of the Balkans.

Remember, Belgrade will always welcome you back with open arms, ready to unveil new discoveries and create more unforgettable experiences. Whether it's your first visit or a return journey, may your adventures in Belgrade continue to inspire and delight.

Thank you for allowing us to be a part of your travel experience. Safe travels, and until we meet again in Belgrade – Srećan put!

Printed in Great Britain
by Amazon